by Aksel James

 HOUGHTON MIFFLIN HARCOURT

PHOTOGRAPHY CREDITS: Cover © Arco Images/Alamy; Toc © Photodisc/Getty Images; 2 © Carl & Ann Purcell/CORBIS; 3 © Photodisc/Getty Images; 4 © Arco Images/Alamy; 5 © Schalke fotografie | Melissa Schalke/Shutterstock; 6 © Zsolt Biczo/Shutterstock

Copyright © by Houghton Mifflin Harcourt Publishing Company

All rights reserved. No part of this work may be reproduced or transmitted in any form or by any means, electronic or mechanical, including photocopying or recording, or by any information storage and retrieval system, without the prior written permission of the copyright owner unless such copying is expressly permitted by federal copyright law. Requests for permission to make copies of any part of the work should be addressed to Houghton Mifflin Harcourt Publishing Company, Attn: Contracts, Copyrights, and Licensing, 9400 South Park Center Loop, Orlando, Florida 32819.

Printed in China

ISBN: 978-0-547-91092-5

10 11 12 13 14 15 0940 21 20 19 18 17 16

4500569761   A B C D E F G

If you have received these materials as examination copies free of charge, Houghton Mifflin Harcourt Publishing Company retains title to the materials and they may not be resold. Resale of examination copies is strictly prohibited.

Possession of this publication in print format does not entitle users to convert this publication, or any portion of it, into electronic format.

The lion can eat.

He can drink.

He can run.

He can play.

He can sleep.
Can I wake him up?
No!

Responding

✓ **WORDS TO KNOW** **Word Builder**

What are some things a lion can do? Use the word "he" in your answer.

✏️ **Write About It**

Text to World Draw a picture of a lion in a zoo. Use vocabulary words to write about your picture.

✓ WORDS TO KNOW

away	must
by	no
he	there

✓ TARGET STRATEGY Monitor/Clarify

Find ways to figure out what doesn't make sense.